Taming
the Lion

First paperback edition
December 2018

ISBN 9781790525522

Published by
Kindle Direct Publishing

Printed in
the United States of America

Dedicated to

my grandparents,

Iqbal Begum,
the late Munir Abbas,
the late Rahmath Unissa
and the late Gulam Mustafa.

{Surah Fatiha}

The poem about

"Truly, in some **POETRY**, there is wisdom."

{Bukhari, Muslim, Abu Dawud}

you

———

Who were you
before they told you
who you couldn't be?

laughing

———

The people
who make you laugh the hardest

also have the saddest stories to tell.

aggravated arson

———

You want me to be
your perfect flame.

Flickering on a candle wick,
bright but contained.

Don't push me too hard
to stay in place.

My lonely fire
can burn your entire house down.

money moves

———

I don't have much money.

I have been told I don't have much beauty.

But my words are my currency,
and I adorn myself in them like gold.

being broke

—

An entire woman

was built

from what these boys

claiming to be men

had broken.

bad boys with good degrees

———

Good on paper,
terrible for my soul.

I could take you home to my father,
but I could never make a home out of you.

good girls with bad choices

Warn your daughters
about the men
that carry sugar
in their mouths,

but hold poison
in their hands.

wild one

———

From her parent's home
to her husband's home.

She always is
supposed to belong to someone
and be someone's burden.

She needs to be "allowed"
to do something.

When she affirms to you
that she belongs
strictly to herself,
and gives permission
for herself,
why would you be taken aback by that?

We only learn
of sweet freedom
during the times we are chained.

spitting and swallowing

———

Here's to ladies
who swallow
lies

but spit out
truth.

her mouth

———

He asked,
"what that mouth do though?"

Speak up.
Tell truth.
Denounce lies.

narcissists

___

You love
to break me
because putting me back together again
is just as thrilling.

nine moons

———

You were born after 9 moons,
stretched an entire womb,
your miracle began
the moment you arrived.

When you break,
which we all do,
it is only always to have you realize
that out of all the fights in the world,
it was you
who was chosen to fight this one.

You were selected to live
and be born,
and you have been chosen for this fight,
even if it means die trying.

broken dreams

———

How many dreams
did we give up for boys
who were nothing
but nightmares?

broken promises

———

If only you knew
the scars you left on my skin
in the places you promised you would touch
but didn't.

leaving

———

There were too many
that wanted to love,

but too little
that wanted to stay.

the war at home

———

We speak on wars
in foreign lands.

But we never speak of the ones
inside of our homes.

breaking me

———

No apologies coming from me,
for everyone who thought they could break me,
I will admit I have given you the impression
that I will always blindly listen.

I have been taught the sweeter the words,
the more you are a slave to their lies.
I am not your savior or your project,
this is me you see, no disguise.

When I walked away when you least suspected
and you wondered, "how could she have known?",
please understand that you have served your purpose
as an unwanted guest inside my home.

You keep telling me I am too strong,
that I am supposed to be quiet and willing,
you tell me that I am too real,
and you intend for it to be insulting.

So no apologies coming from me,
my fire was too ferocious for your water,
if you really wanted to kill me,
you should have come with something stronger.

father feminism

———

My father

taught me feminism

when he taught me

that I am more

before they started teaching me

that I was less.

colonialism

———

Brown girls
spiced with turmeric,
coloured with tamarind.

To have been told she isn't beautiful,
since she is not white sugar.

Her eyes are not green or blue,
but are dark and deep.

She will drown you in her ocean of stories
and make you gasp for water
when you taste her.

robes and rags

———

Righteousness
is not reserved for anyone.

I know devils
dressed in religious robes
that kill souls.

And I know angels
wearing rags
that save them.

leadership's entourage

Called me so many names
butchered my name like slaughter,
wash your mouth out with some soap
and call that holy water.

Call out leadership for hypocrisy
got called a drama starter,
so tell me is it still drama
if they could hurt your son or daughter?

Silence me, silence all of us.
Put your hand on me, put a hand on all of us.

Oh you're not about violence?
Well I'm not about silence.
I'm going to take this car called Justice
and put on some mad mileage.

Swerve in and out of lanes
only brake if I catch a light,
only time I take a seat
is when I kneel for what's right.

The title you gave me is for flatter.
The label you gave me won't make me shatter.
The names you call me really don't matter.
Your insults are all over the place, paint splatter.
Can't box me in with the former or latter.

Breathe.

That was too many rhymes,
not a ghostwriter but I can give you lines.

So take this right here
use it to feel empowered
Never let them knock you down,
be a hero, not a coward.

what is wrong with the youth

—

How many bodies must we bury?

How many caskets must we carry
until you realize your actions
are carried in the blood of your children?

So when you mourn the souls of the youth,
do not forget their roots
are nourished on your soil.

why you should write

———

Write about home
and how sometimes it isn't.

Write letters to the person who tore you apart,
you will not be interrupted with their excuses.

Write requests for freedom,
and how being yourself will set you free
but society always keeps you prisoner.

Write pieces on how you never feel beautiful,
and how mirrors remind you of this.

Write how your mother's words are what you inherit.

Write your father's dreams, praising him for the ones he
accomplished
and the ones you will finish.

Write for your children
the questions they will have for you
and the answers you are ashamed of.

Write what you know,
and what you wish for them to know too.

evil expectations

———

Please
do not talk to me
about the hellfire
when you make
people's lives
a living hell.

trying too hard

———

Step one
of trying to get them to love you.

Don't.

Never trade all of you
for just a piece of them.

truth or dare

———

God and I
play truth or dare.

He knows my truths already
and He dares me with them daily.

pain in silence

———

To be hurt but be heard.

Pain has more words
than happy.

This is why I go quiet when I am hurting.

My pen will speak my words
and my voice will write in silence.

coming back

———

You tell me you need me
when I am serious about leaving.

You love the leaves
only when they are falling.

You didn't love the tree
when it gave you shade.

You realized its beauty
only when the colors changed.

But remember the season
that comes after the fall,
everything becomes cold
and dies
only to be born again.

side chicks

———

I can no longer
be a cure
for your temporary loneliness

when I made you
a permanent cure
for mine.

all these rhymes

What do I know about pain?

Like a butcher knows meat,
like Khabib knows winning,
like Dr. Dre knows a beat.

I can quote Iqbal and Rumi
but serve Tupac rhymes,
you can try to box me in
but I don't color in the lines.

God told me to pay my dues
and He's collected the fines,
dig all the dirt you want
but diamonds still shine.

being real

———

Realness is such a rarity
that it is often mistaken for illness.

the knife that cuts the worst

—

You cannot claim
God has your back
as you take a dagger
and stab the backs
of God's creation.

what you will never be

———

I am going to be
what you never could be.

Happy for me.

invitations

———

She didn't ask for it.

How can there be answers
to the questions
that were never said?

what she wore

___

They asked her
what she was wearing.

She was wearing legs he opened
even though she screamed no.

She was wearing arms
that were pushing him away.

She was wearing teeth
that tried to bite and disarm him
but he stuffed it closed.

She was wearing a voice
that could not scream
because he held a knife and said he would kill her.

You asked her
what she was wearing.

She was dressed in a soul
but you cannot find yours.

testimony

———

I believe her

because they did not believe me.

battle scars

———

Not all scars
show wounds.

The deepest cuts
make our hearts bleed.

those taught to hate their names and skin

———

My hair is so black
it's blue.
But I dyed it blonde and brown
hoping to look like Kathy and Sandy.

I took my dark eye color
and made it green with contacts
that made my eyes itch.

What about my name?
"Ashley, call me Ashley", I say.
I want to look like them
and be like them.

I'll let them call me whatever is easier for them.
The name my mother gave me has no place here.

I die to be accepted.

I don't want these features that he doesn't want.
I don't want this name they can't pronounce.

I don't want to remind him of his mother.
I want to remind him of the girls on TV,
the ones
that don't look
anything like me.

After being born again into the body I was given
I learned that my looks are not just memorable,
my name is.

Black hair, dark eyes, dusky skin.
How could I not see the royalty in me?

Not even the sun dares to burns me.

death by poison

———

If you knew
that the food you love
had a single drop of poison
would you take your chances and eat it?

So tell me
why you keep going back to them
when you know
they have poisoned you
every single time?

sons and mothers

———

He married the girl of his dreams
just like his mother,
from a land and culture
that taught her she couldn't do better.

He grew up hating the fact
that his mother
was so dependent on his father.

But he loved the fact
that there were other women
just like her.

daughters and fathers

———

You cannot demand
for strong daughters
when you like their mothers
to be weak.

the light

———

The light you carry
will intimidate their darkness.

Do you know
just how much larger
the sun is
than the moon?

the dark place

———

Don't blame me
for the things I did
when I was in a very dark place.

I held on to anything and everything
that made me feel less alone.

misery's company

———

I did not come this far
to hold the hands of anyone
that wants to take me back
to the dark place I met them in
just so they can have some company.

roses

———

Every rose
that is real
came from dirt
that is real too.

taming the lion

———

The lion
does not need to roar
for you to be afraid.

Perhaps
you cannot hear me
because you fear
standing close.

butterflies

———

No one curses a butterfly
that takes flight
after being cocooned
and only able to crawl.

So if you choose to leave,
do not just go.

Do not walk.
Don't even run.
Fly.

how to kill a dragon

———

Please do not say
your purpose is to protect me.

I have slayed dragons
without even a sword.

You must provide me
with something I cannot give myself,
perhaps a piece
of a peace
of mind.

reflections

————

I learned true love
when I looked into a mirror
and I said to myself,

"you are more than enough,
you are everything,
and that is why
it's going to be okay."

the throne

I built a castle
inside of you
but some crowns
outgrow their thrones.

So when you leave
because some kings
become treacherous

I am still queen.

mean girls

———

I am sorry
I am selective
with where I choose to fight.

It's not because
you are not worth fighting for,
but because I know how important it is
for you to be right.

I know this may be your only one
so take this victory,
petty has no place here
in the hearts of those making history.

child's play

———

Just like you let a child
win in a game,
you must allow some people
to believe they are victorious.

We let the children play on the floor
and the real warriors go to war.

calling you

———

My calling

is greater

than calling you

and asking you

to see my greatness.

word wars

———

I have fought
so many wars against myself
that if someone comes for me
it is merely practice.

Your words are just the ones I use
to write masterpieces.

perfection

You have a preference
for perfection.

You wanted roses without the thorns.
You wanted starry skies without the darkness.
You wanted woman without the woe.

I remain deeply devoted
to all my flaws.

So if you decide to point them out
in an attempt to remind me
of how incomplete I come,
I will kindly remind you
that you saw something in me
that you did not see in you.

So am I undone or are you?

what we attract

Where on her does it say
use as you please
and leave as you came?

Did you see the broken home,
and the broken family
and think that you could get away
with breaking her heart?

children at the wall

When you close your borders to children
in bizarre hopes of securing those borders
from monsters,

tell me
who is a greater monster
than the one who tells a child
that their dreams are invalid
because of where they call home?

beyond the wall

————

Bring my child
back into my womb's waters
I will jail them
for another nine brutal moons
if it means
that you will not take them
and separate them
in a land I thought
they would be free in.

liberation

———

You
are not there to liberate us.

Freedom
is never won in war.

Mothers
will always be shackled to the land
they have buried their children in.

God listening

———

What matters is when night falls
and the world is fast asleep,
I cup my hands because God calls
and I remember I am not weak.

For it is He who knows everything
and He who knows what's in my soul,
I am the writer of this song I sing,
a story only He has ever been told.

hot sauce

———

One generation removed
from a child bride,
from apartheid,
from a white side
and a black side,
from laws we had to protest
that we refused to abide.

You want to sit here
and tell me I should be thankful
that I don't have my hands full
with five children by the age of 20
and that I should be grateful
that I'm still in this country.

But I built this right here
off your hate mongering fear,
I don't need to say thank you for ish
and stop frisking me at the airport
when my papers legit.

And stop asking me if my food is spicy when I bring it around,
as much as you appropriate my culture
you'll never be brown
and you'll never be down,
will never know what it's like,
to be told you aren't beautiful
because you're not white.

You're not about this movement
as much as you say you are.
I don't need you to tell me this country has come far.

Everything I am and everything I'll ever be
is because of who I am
not because of this country.

schools

———

Bullets and barrels
over books and blood.

You want to arm us with what takes a life
and take away from what saves them.

(December 14ᵗʰ, 2012: 20 children under the age of 8 years old and a number of faculty protecting their babies at Sandy Hook Elementary School were brutally murdered)

(February 14ᵗʰ, 2018: 14 teenagers under the age of 19 and a number of faculty protecting their students at Stoneman Douglas High School were violently murdered)

(Countless other schools and places of education have become places of violence, much of which could have been prevented by firearm regulation)

fighting fists

———

Kneel.

Because when the anthem is sung
and the flags are waved,
God knows we are not free
but He knows we are brave.

brown skin

———

To dark, brown skin
that you learned
to be ashamed of.

Your skin
does not burn in the sun.

How could you hate
what God's rays
embrace with love?

finding yourself where you lost it and not in India, Italy or Indonesia

———

People travel the world
trying to find themselves.

So they get lost

on paths unknown,
in places they can't pronounce,
and meet with people
they do not know.

But tell me,
how can you find yourself
if you're looking everywhere
except for in the place
where you left it?

sarees

———

Mothers drape their daughters
similar to how their mothers did,
pleated and carefully draped,
the fall cascading over their shoulders.

There are two things
Indian mothers pass on to their daughters,
their sarees
and their gold.

Do you know how many stories
are told in these two things?
An entire history.
An entire lineage and ancestry.

And every daughter thinks
when she wears what her mother wore,
what stories will she get to tell her daughter
when she adorns her in gold and silk fabric too.

loud women

———

Be weary of those who were
comfortable in your silence.

Your voice will wake their demons
that were disguised as kings.

queens

———

Queens
don't get off their thrones
to address peasants.

So if they come for you
let them come.

A kingdom's doors
will always have beggars outside
just begging
for a royal to listen.

your worth

———

Your magnificence
was forgotten.

His food
was your vulnerability.

When he told you sweet lies
and gave you fairy tales coupled with gifts
you got so little,
mistook it for so much.

You thought you found your forever,
but when he left,
you felt it all.
You cried so much
and had an empty soul for months.

You then became angry and plead,
"Don't leave",
as if he would listen.

When a man makes up his mind
he has made up his mind.

Please don't go back to someone
who made you forget you
and who you were
and made you think
that all you were was for him.

My love, you are so much more.

lovers at night

———

At the end
of every day

I really hope
you're still in love
with you.

the best lessons

———

You remind me
that the best lessons

are learned from the worst people.

weaponry

My words are my weapons,
draw my guns only if I need them,
I can shoot blanks and make you run,
if I shoot bullets consider yourself done.

You keep saying these words hoping for attention,
you keep writing paragraphs and don't even get a mention,
you create so much but not a single masterpiece,
so many lines you spit, but not even a conversation piece.

Keep using your words to hate hoping that it reaches,
this ink I write is like blood, they suck it up like leeches,
I almost put the pen down, but I remembered this is a gift,
my words are my weapons, so I write now with a closed fist.

birthing broken girls

———

There has always been a burden
with being born.

A little girl that is broken
becomes the grown woman scorned.

staying warm

———

Some of us
exude such a fire

that some of us
will come around
just to feel the warmth.

pieces of meat

He tells me women like me
are rotten.

A low hanging fruit you cannot eat.
A flower that is a weed.

Men do not want sad and strong,
they want happy but weak.

They don't want old scars
that are stitched up with grief.

Men want fresh meat.

So I sit here cutting every part of my limbs
and keep offering it to him.

"Is this good?"
He says, "no, I want blood."
I prepare my heart extra rare for him, a true treat.

He declines and says,
it is not enough.
I could give you the world,
it's not enough.
Soft and pretty, every single fantasy you could want.

N o t
E n o u g h.

"What do you event want?" I ask him
with my mouth and lips on the floor.

"Not you", he responds
to all of the parts left of me that he did not want.

So I become rotten
like meat left out in the open.

taking an L

———

Love and loss.

Four letter words
beginning with the same letter.

But so is lust.

lemonade

———

Life made me bitter

but so are the skins
that cover the fruit
that makes lemonade.

the cure

————

I am not roses.

I am poison ivy, a Venus fly trap.

I am something they tell you to stay away from,
don't touch, just look at.

You cannot make me into water,
my petals won't make you pretty.

My leaves will capture you whole
leaving you itching and yearning
for the cure.

being single

—

You are worth so much more
than having to wait on bended knee
for someone to love you back.

being ashamed

———

Do not be ashamed of your story.

Being relatable is a great gift
only few are chosen to receive.

being enough

———

I will always
be too much

for the people
that aren't enough.

battered woman's battle

———

At least he says good morning,
although I did not know where he was last night.

At least he texts back after one week,
he could have just gone ghost.

At least he comes home,
shirt undone, smelling of another woman's perfume,
he came home to me after all.

At least he lets me go out,
he just has to pick and choose with whom and where.

At least he got me roses on Valentine's Day,
but he gave me a black eye on my birthday.

At least he says he loves me,
it's like walking on egg shells though,
sometimes he says he hates me.

At least he didn't hit me,
just called me ugly and a nobody.

At least he didn't kill me,
he just beat me blue and bloody.

double standards

———

The boy
is allowed to claim many bodies.

He is not burdened
with the miracle of a womb in water.

The boy is rewarded immensely
each time he leaves his mark.

And the girl?

She lowers the number of bodies she has touched willingly.

She would rather say the number of the ones
whom she did not give permission.

profit prophet

———

A poet that demands profit
is like a prophet without poems.

Only a liar will thirst for money
for people to hear false truth.

breathing heavy

———

I let go of me
to let you in.

Your water cooled my fire,
but there was still the smoke.

Inhaling it
is what killed me.

speaking in screams

———

Your silence

screams to me

all of the things

that I could not hear

when you were speaking.

deep love

———

Here is the problem
with people
who love so deeply.

They love so much
that they forget how to love themselves.

They unlearn all they know
to learn all of you.

grandmothers

———

Do you ever wonder
how they did it?

Our grandmothers.

With nothing but husbands handed to them.

They were told to make an entire life
out of a red dress and henna stained palms.

It was an entirely different reason
to cry in those times.
The ceremony of leaving all you know behind
and having to graciously accept all of the unknown.

The cooking pots they found friendships with
in places they had never visited before
prior to the day they became women.

The children they bore
in tiny rooms with other women
who knew the pain
but didn't speak of it.

Do you wonder what it was like
for our grandmothers to bathe in waters foreign,
and to learn of tragedies through letters
sent too late?

Rarely returning home
to all the comforts they knew
to make a better life
for you.

the map to my mother

———

My mother's face
is a map I hold
it tells me how to reach
to the woman that she is

but I know
I will only reach
halfway.

every woman I know

———

I am in love with every single woman I know.

We bear burden like it is our purpose.
We happily mistake our pain for pleasure.

Us women deal with so much,
we scold one another for dealing with that much.

We carry the sun yet still care of the moon in stormy skies.

Our hearts break easily because of the weight they hold.

The soul of a woman becomes a ghost when it is treated as if it is
dead already.

That is why I am in love with every single woman I know.

To stand here,
and look at you
and seeing that you still persevere
it is the loveliest thing I know.

humankind inc.

I don't hold humans accountable anymore.

For war.
For injustice.
For hate.

There is no standard for the dead
that mingle amongst the living.

storms she weathers

———

Tell every storm
I have bathed in her already.

Every mountain that you fear
I have climbed already.

Burnt bridges
just to break the connection,
built alliances
with people I cannot mention.

I am half my mother
and half my father.

I inherited struggle
and all of its company.

Do you know whose blood runs here?
Royalty.

I am the queen of my own destiny.

holding hands

———

Whenever I held a hand
I thought they would lead me
to where I needed to go.

My hands stopped tracing the map in yours.
I could have found my way to where I was going
with more faith in myself and less in you.

standing still

———

I cannot hold still.

A candle's scent will fill a room
only if the flame dances.

falling apart

———

When you fall apart,
understand that every piece
that breaks off
is one more piece
to build something stronger.

humility

———

"You need to be humbled."

But how?

No one needs to be humbled.

There is nothing more humbling
than knowing that your breath
is simply borrowed.

Tupac's truth and Rumi's religion

———

The truth never has many followers.

So don't boast your numbers
when I have letters.

Aren't we still quoting Rumi on spirituality?
And still captioning photos with Tupac's rhymes about reality?

steps

———

Sometimes the bravest step we take
is the one we decide not to.

your opinions

——

I do not care
to change your opinion of me.

There is too much to change in the world.

I would rather find a voice
for the billions who do not have one,
than to ever try to find my voice
with you.

the night you died

———

Here is to dark nights
you thought
you would die in.

May they always
allow you to remember
why you live.

privilege

——

Pretty made them stare
but it did not make them stay.

There is no privilege in pretty
when we all bleed the same.

the joker

———

I am asked what happened and what is wrong
almost all the time.

I am a liar when I tell you
that everything is fine.

I have learned the same things many are taught
to stay silent and still, adorned in fabrics to cover up what hurts.

These clothes no longer fit.

There are stories in these scars
that scare the ones that don't belong here.

dirty dead secrets

—

A writer's
greatest secret
is the subject
of their sadness.

All of our ex lovers are buried alive-
but in words.

missing on a milk carton

———

I do miss you.
But I miss the person I was before you even more.

grown girls

———

I am
too much woman

to be your
ideal girl.

knowing nothing

———

There are many stories
between   the   words   I   say

I wish you had known them
before you replied to me with,
"you know nothing".

history

———

I am a solider to my history
I don't regret but simply learn,
although I have encountered misery,
the smoke choked me
but I did not burn.

becoming

In the deep dark words of mystery
where witches and ghosts lie,
I have walked through the forest's treachery
and found peace where I thought I would die.

The cruel and unusual wind has blown
with its breath fierce and strong,
I feel comfort inside a danger zone
and found where I belong.

tears that tear us apart

———

Thank you
to every heartbreak.

Every tear
created a word.

strong women on demand

———

How do I become the woman you want

and then change back to the woman I am
but only when you need me to be?

the end

———

You assume it is the end.

You believe there won't be another like him or her so you hold on to
all the good.
You so badly want to think it is not your fault and that this is all
just a great misunderstanding and it can salvaged.
Sometimes you cave in, you pick up the phone and you let them know
that they are on your mind.
You want them to know they are not forgotten, that you still pine for
their affection,
that you are happy to give so much for so little.

This is where you break.

You lose touch, you lose sight of who you are.
Like a costume, you assume a new character everyday
hoping that they will love one of the many masks you wear.

But didn't they tell you that you can't change who you are to make
them want you?

They have already decided that you cannot fit into their space.
Now comes the battle of fitting a square into a circle.
To be accommodated, you are cutting off your corners and sacrificing
your circulation.
Yes, love is compromise but it is not a means to disguise.

If he or she falls in love with your mask, they will keep asking you to
wear another.

So instead of fighting for the one that didn't stay,
find the one that will fall in love with your current face.

Don't hide who you are for what they can never be-

yours.

sorry

———

What I have to say
won't always be pretty.

My mouth is filled with roses
that still have thorns.

me

———

How many portraits

did you paint of me

before you realized

you were using the wrong colors?

about the author

Aishah S. Gulam is a Muslim Indian-American writer, poet and advocate.

She lives in the United States in Michigan where she was born and raised.

Made in the USA
Middletown, DE
15 January 2019